Atlas of Plants

Created by Gallimard Jeunesse,
Claude Delafosse,
and Sylvaine Perols
Illustrated by Sylvaine Perols

A FIRST DISCOVERY BOOK

Note: Atlas of Plants is a child's very first atlas.
Using simplified maps, bright illustrations, and basic
information, it introduces young children to the
diversity of plant life all over the world.

Cartwheel
·B·O·O·K·S·®

SCHOLASTIC INC.
New York   Toronto   London   Auckland   Sydney

North America and Central America

One of the oldest living trees is the giant sequoia, which grows in California.

There are many varieties of the poppy. Some grow wild in fields.

The saguaro is a giant cactus that grows in the deserts of Arizona, Mexico, and California.

The bald cypress tree grows in swampy areas. Most cypress trees are evergreens.

The California poppy, usually golden yellow, may also be orange, pink, or white.

The bases of some giant sequoias are as wide as some city streets — over 35 feet!

The bald cypress grows "knees," which stick up from the water and supply air to the tree's roots.

The saguaro's branches store water. Animals are attracted to its flowers and to holes in its trunk.

North America

The leaves and seeds of the maple tree grow in pairs. The winged seeds are called keys.

The pink flowers of the blueberry plant produce juicy fruit, used to make jelly.

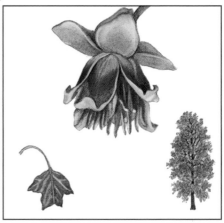

Over one third of the world's pine trees are found in North America.

The tulip tree is easy to identify. It has greenish, tulip-shaped flowers.

North and South America

The potato is not a fruit or root. It is really a large underground stem.

Yucca plants can be small shrubs or large trees. Their flowers are bell-shaped.

There are 20,000 kinds of orchids. Most grow on rocks or the branches and trunks of trees.

The tomato is really a fruit— not a vegetable. It is the most widely grown fruit in the world.

South America

The cacao is an evergreen tree.
Chocolate is made from
roasted cacao beans.

Lianas are tropical vines
that cling tightly to the trunks
and branches of trees.

The tillandsia has no true roots.
It grows on tree branches.

The corn plant is a member
of the grass family.

Lianas twist themselves upwards and sometimes completely smother their host tree.

The cacao flower and fruit grow out of the tree trunk. Cacao beans are found inside the fruit.

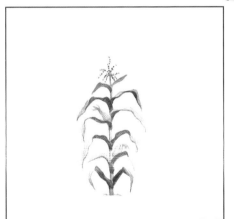

An ear of corn is the fruit of the corn plant.

Sometimes, small animals live within the leaves of the tillandsia.

Africa

Many date palms grow in oases in the desert. They provide food and shade.

The welwitschia begins with two long leaves. As it ages, they split into many pieces.

Egypt is one of Africa's major cotton-growing countries. Cotton is mostly grown in the hot regions.

The baobab tree grows in the savanna. Its huge trunk stores water.

The welwitschia can live to be 2,000 years old. The female plants grow red cone clusters.

Dates grow on stalks in big bunches. Some single bunches can hold over a thousand dates.

The baobab flower opens in the evening. The tree loses its leaves during the dry season.

The cotton flower produces a seed pod called a boll. White fibers, used to make cloth, grow from the seeds.

Africa

The long leaves of the traveller's palm of Madagascar catch and hold rainwater.

Acacia trees grow in tropical areas such as the African savanna.

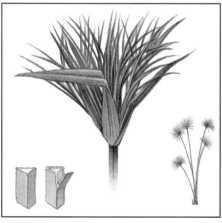

The coffee plant's berries each have two seeds or beans. Roasted beans make coffee.

Papyrus plants grow in northern and tropical Africa. The inner part of the stem is used to make paper.

Europe

The woodland strawberry has a delicate smell. Its seeds grow on the outside of the fruit.

The wood of an olive tree is very hard. The fruit is eaten or used to make olive oil.

The English oak produces acorns that are eaten by many animals.

The flower of the bee orchid looks like a female bumblebee. It attracts male bumblebees.

Europe

There are about a dozen kinds of chestnut trees, valued for their fruit and strong wood.

The English daisy blooms almost all year long in meadows and along roadsides.

The bulrush, also called cattail, is found along the edges of streams and ponds.

The wild apple tree belongs to the rose family. There are over two dozen kinds of wild apples.

It's easy to spot the English daisy. It has white-and-rose-colored petals and a gold center.

The fruit of the chestnut tree, the nuts, develop inside spiny burs that grow on the tree.

The apple tree blooms in spring.
Its fruit ripens in summer.

The brown flower spikes of the bulrush are easy to see against the dark green leaves.

Siberia

The Siberian fir is a big evergreen. Its wood is used to build houses.

Labrador tea is a small evergreen that bears little, white, sweet-smelling flowers.

The mountain cranberry produces bright red berries that ripen at the end of summer.

The downy birch is found in the forests that border the icy tundra.

Northern Asia

Most rhododendrons in the
wild grow in moist
mountain areas.

The gingko was first grown
in China. The female tree
bears a stinky-smelling fruit.

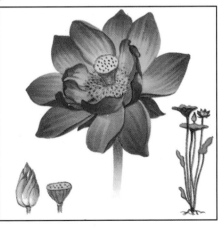

The apricot tree originated in
East Asia. Its fruit,
the apricot, contains a large pit.

In India, the lotus
is considered
a sacred plant.

Southern Asia

The pitcher plant gets minerals
it needs from decaying insects
trapped in its pitcher.

Bamboo is a giant grass.
Pandas live in bamboo forests
in China.

Rice has been grown
in flooded rice fields
in China for 7,000 years.

The banana plant is grown in
tropical areas such as Malaysia.
Bananas are very nutritious fruits.

Bamboo has a strong, hollow stem, used to make furniture and paper.

Insects are attracted by the bright colors and nectar of the pitcher plant.

The banana shoot produces one crop of bananas, and then dies.

Rice plants sprout just days after planting. The heads of mature plants hold rice kernels.

Australia and Oceania

The coconut tree is often
found in the wild
along sea coasts.

The spine bush of the
red desert of Australia
forms bristly clumps.

The eucalyptus tree
comes from Australia.
Koalas feed only on these trees.

Mangrove trees grow along
the coasts of many tropical
oceans and rivers.

The spine bush is a fortress of tough leaves. Animals make their homes inside.

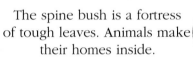

The coconut seed is surrounded by a thick, hard husk. Inside is a liquid called coconut milk.

The thick roots of the mangrove make a good breeding ground for fish and other marine animals.

The leaves of the eucalyptus tree produce a valuable oil.

The bougainvillea may be a shrub or vine. It has very small flowers.

The papaya is a fleshy seed fruit that grows in tropical climates.

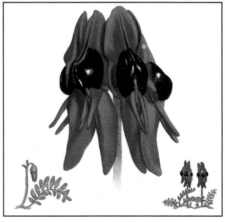

The xanthorrhoea, or grass tree, produces tufts of thin leaves on top of its stem.

The unique flowers of the desert pea appear during the winter in Australia.

The Arctic

All kinds of medicines
are made from the
mosslike ground pine.

The arctic poppy grows
on the tundra during
the brief arctic summer.

Small white flowers and
clusters of bright red fruit
make up the arctic bramble.

The dwarf birch, with its tiny
thick leaves, is one of the few
trees that grows in the arctic.

All of these plants hold a record!

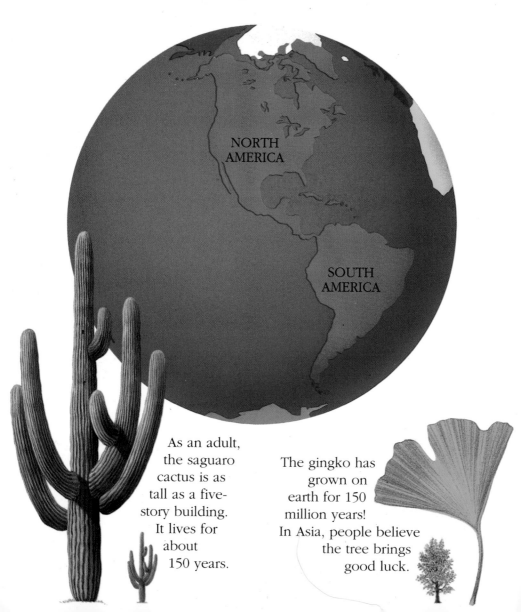

NORTH AMERICA

SOUTH AMERICA

As an adult, the saguaro cactus is as tall as a five-story building. It lives for about 150 years.

The gingko has grown on earth for 150 million years! In Asia, people believe the tree brings good luck.